AIRBORNE RANGERS

by Michael Burgan

Consultant:
Major William T. James, Jr.
Regimental S5
75th Ranger Regiment

CAPSTONE BOOKS

an imprint of Capstone Press
Mankato, Minnesota

Capstone Books are published by Capstone Press
151 Good Counsel Drive, P. O. Box 669, Mankato, Minnesota 56002
http://www.capstone-press.com

Library of Congress Cataloging-in-Publication Data
Burgan, Michael.
    U.S. Army special forces: airborne rangers/by Michael Burgan.
    p. cm.—(Warfare and weapons)
    Includes bibliographical references (p. 44) and index.
    Summary: Introduces the U.S. Army's Airborne Rangers, their history, mission,
development, training, and equipment.
    ISBN 0-7368-0337-8
    1. United States. Army—Commando troops Juvenile literature. 2. United
States. Army—Airborne troops—Juvenile literature. 3. Special forces (Military
science)—United States—Juvenile literature. [1. United States. Army—Airborne
troops. 2. United States. Army—Commando troops. 3. Special forces (Military
science)] I. Title. II. Series
UA34.R36B87 2000
356'.167—dc21   99-23155
                                                                   CIP

Editorial Credits
Blake Hoena, editor; Timothy Halldin, cover designer; Linda Clavel, illustrator;
    Heidi Schoof, photo researcher

Photo Credits
Corbis, 18
Corbis/Bettmann, 15
Corbis/Hulton-Deutsch Collection, 16
David Bohrer, cover, 9, 12, 24, 27, 28, 30, 34, 37, 40, 43
Defense Visual Information Center, 4, 20
Photri-Microstock, 7

**Special thanks to David Bohrer, Pulitzer Prize-winning photographer for the
Los Angeles Times, for providing the cover and interior photos.**

Table of Contents

Features

Chapter 1

Airborne Rangers

On October 3, 1993, Somalian soldiers shot down two U.S. Army Blackhawk helicopters. These helicopters crashed in the city of Mogadishu, Somalia. The helicopters were carrying Airborne Rangers sent to capture a group of Somalian warlords. These military leaders were responsible for attacks against the Somalian people.

A battle followed. Somalian soldiers attacked the Rangers who were traveling in these two helicopters. The U.S. military sent more Rangers to help. These Rangers also were sent to recover the wounded and dead U.S. soldiers.

This is a Blackhawk helicopter. Rangers traveled in Blackhawk helicopters during missions in Somalia.

The Rangers had to fight to rescue their fellow Rangers. The Somalian soldiers attacked the Rangers with rockets and machine guns. The Rangers returned fire and finally reached safety. Six Rangers died in the fighting. The Rangers killed more than 500 enemy soldiers.

"Rangers Lead the Way"

Rangers are specially trained members of the U.S. Army. They are trained to enter battle scenes quickly and quietly. They also are called Airborne Rangers. All Rangers are trained as paratroopers. They sometimes reach battle sites by jumping out of aircraft using parachutes. These large pieces of strong, light cloth allow Rangers to float safely to the ground.

Rangers often are the first U.S. soldiers to arrive at battle sites. Their motto is "Rangers lead the way." Rangers gather information about enemy forces. This helps other U.S. military forces prepare to enter battle sites.

Rangers are trained to jump out of aircraft using parachutes.

The 75th Ranger Regiment

The U.S. Army has about 2,000 Rangers. They are divided into three units called battalions. The 1st Battalion is based at Hunter Army Airfield in Savannah, Georgia. The 2nd Battalion is at Fort Lewis, Washington. The 3rd Battalion is based at Fort Benning, Georgia. Combined, these three battalions are called a regiment. They make up the 75th Ranger Regiment.

The 75th Ranger Regiment is an infantry regiment. Infantry unit members are trained to fight on the ground. Rangers also are called light infantry. They do not use tanks or other large weapons to support them in battle. They carry all of their own weapons and equipment. Some people consider Rangers the world's best light infantry force.

Ranger Duties

Rangers perform a variety of missions when they reach battle sites. Rangers sometimes are sent to capture enemy airfields. U.S. military pilots then can use these airfields to land their

Infantry units fight on the ground.

aircraft. These aircraft bring more troops and supplies to battle sites. Rangers also may scout enemy territory for enemy forces.

Rangers can be ready for duty anywhere in the world with 18 hours' notice. Rangers often train in deserts, jungles, and on mountains. This prepares them for duty in different parts of the world. Some training missions even appear to be real missions. Rangers are not told that these missions are practice missions. This prepares Rangers to be ready for duty at all times.

Sun: The sun represents the battles during which Rangers and Chinese soldiers fought together against Japanese soldiers; China's flag had a sun on it during World War II.

Star: The star stands for the star on Burma's flag; Merrill's Marauders did much of their fighting in Burma.

Lightning bolt: The lightning bolt stands for the speed at which Rangers perform their duties.

Colors: Each color represents a team of Rangers that fought during World War II; these teams were units in Merrill's Marauders and were named after these colors; the teams were red, white, blue, and green.

Chapter 2

A Long History

Soldiers called Rangers first fought in North America more than 300 years ago. Their weapons and equipment were simple compared to those used today. But today's Rangers perform some of the same duties as the first Rangers.

The First Rangers

In the 1600s, the first British settlers arrived in North America. They often battled the native peoples who lived there. But these American Indians fought differently than the British. The British learned that they could not use large armies to fight. American Indians did not fight in large, open battlefields like Europeans. Instead, American Indians fought in small groups. These groups could quietly and

Today's Rangers are trained to sneak through the wilderness and fight in small groups.

quickly move through the wilderness and attack by surprise.

To battle the American Indians, the British learned to fight in small groups. They then could sneak up on the American Indians and raid their campsites. Afterward, the British were able to quickly flee before they could be caught. British soldiers often said they "ranged" as they looked for American Indians. They sometimes traveled many miles in a single day. These soldiers were the first Rangers.

In 1756, Great Britain was fighting in the French and Indian War (1754–1763). American colonists formed Ranger units to help the British fight the French and the American Indians. These units were called Rogers' Rangers. Their leader was Robert Rogers. His Rangers traveled through the woods searching for the enemy. They carried few supplies. This helped them move quickly. They also used sleds and ice skates to continue searching for the enemy soldiers during winter.

Robert Rogers led Ranger units during the French and Indian War.

Rangers took part in the D-Day invasion.

Early American Wars

American colonists again formed units of
Rangers during the Revolutionary War
(1775–1783). This time, the enemy was Great
Britain. The American colonists were fighting
to free themselves from British rule. They
wanted to form their own country.

Rangers often acted as reconnaissance (ree-KAH-nuh-sinss) forces. They travelled ahead of the main army to look for British troops. They watched the British troops' actions and reported back to their leaders with this information.

Rangers also fought in the Civil War (1861–1865). Both the United States and the Confederate States had Rangers. But the most famous Rangers were Mosby's Rangers. Their leader was John Mosby. He and his Rangers were members of the Confederate army. They often sneaked into land controlled by the United States. They then blew up train lines and raided enemy camps.

World War II and Korea

During World War II (1939–1945), the U.S. government created new Ranger units. These soldiers learned to fight from English commandos. Commandos are highly trained soldiers who work in small groups. They move into battle sites ahead of the main military. They often spy on enemy forces.

Frank Merrill led units of Rangers against the Japanese during World War II.

Rangers helped win many important battles in Europe and North Africa during World War II. On June 6th, 1944, Rangers led U.S. troops into battle at Normandy, France. This invasion was called D-Day. It was the largest land invasion of World War II.

Another group of Rangers was called Merrill's Marauders. Their leader was Brigadier General Frank Merrill. During World War II, they fought in the jungles of Burma in

Asia. They traveled almost 1,000 miles (1,600 kilometers) on foot through these jungles. They won many battles against Japanese soldiers.

Rangers also fought in the Korean War (1950–1953). They sometimes used parachutes to reach battle sites. They also trained in small boats. Once again, the Rangers fought ahead of the main U.S. Army units. They performed reconnaissance missions and raided enemy camps.

From the Vietnam War to Today

New Ranger units formed during the Vietnam War (1954–1975). The army added Long Range Patrol Companies (LRPs). LRPs were specifically trained for reconnaissance. They were trained as paratroopers. They also entered and left battle sites by helicopters.

Two of today's Ranger battalions formed in 1974. At this time, Rangers became a permanent part of the U.S. Army. In the past, the army did not have active Ranger units when the United States was not at war. The army formed a third battalion in 1984. These three battalions now form the 75th Ranger Regiment.

The 75th Ranger Regiment has fought many times since 1974. Its first mission involved the failed Iranian hostage rescue attempt in 1980. Rangers were sent to rescue U.S. citizens that were held against their will in Iran.

In 1983, Rangers fought in Grenada. U.S. troops were sent to this Caribbean island to protect U.S. medical students. Rebels had overthrown the Grenadian government. The U.S. government thought the rebels might harm the medical students in Grenada.

Rangers used parachutes to land at Point Salines airport on Grenada. They made the runways safe for U.S. military planes to land. They cleared the runways of any objects such as vehicles that could stop planes from landing. The Rangers also protected the planes from enemy attacks.

In 1989, the Rangers fought in Panama during Operation Just Cause. Once again, their mission was to arrive before the main U.S. Armed Forces. During the night, Rangers dropped by parachute from airplanes. They took control of Panama's main airports. They also captured the Panamanian Army's main headquarters.

Rangers sometimes parachute to mission sites at night.

Mission

Operation: Restore Hope

Date: October 3, 1993

Location: Mogadishu, Somalia

Situation: Somalian warlords were responsible for attacks against the Somalian people. The U.S. military sent Rangers to capture the warlords. Rangers traveled in Blackhawk helicopters to the warlords' headquarters.

Airborne Rangers: During the mission, the warlords' soldiers attacked U.S. troops with machine guns and rockets. These soldiers shot down two Blackhawk helicopters carrying Rangers.

Rescue: More Rangers were sent to help recover the wounded and dead soldiers. The Rangers had to fight the warlords' troops to reach the crashed helicopters. The battle lasted for several hours. In the end, the Rangers killed more than 500 enemy troops. Six Rangers died in the battle. All the wounded and dead U.S. soldiers were recovered.

KENYA

Lake Victoria

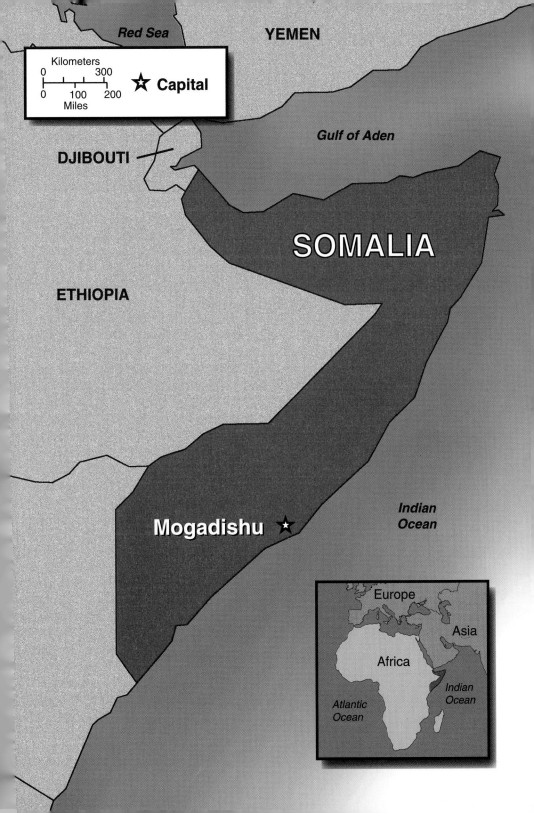

Chapter 3

Training

Each year, about 2,700 soldiers begin Ranger training. Almost 1,000 fail. The training is very difficult. In battle, Rangers must be able to fight on all kinds of terrain. These areas of land include jungles, deserts, and mountains. Rangers often have to go days with little food or sleep. Ranger training creates these same conditions for trainees.

First Steps
Rangers receive their basic training at Fort Benning, Georgia. The soldiers in the Ranger training course come from all branches of the U.S. military. They may be from the navy, air force, or marines. But most are from the U.S. Army.

Training creates the same conditions that Rangers must work under when performing real missions.

All soldiers in Ranger training are volunteers. These soldiers ask to become Rangers. Many already are paratroopers. Trainees must be able to parachute from an airplane by the time they finish school.

Only men can become Rangers. Congressional law does not allow women to enter ground combat specialties. These jobs may involve duties that need to be performed while under direct fire from enemy forces.

Some soldiers take a special class to prepare for Ranger training. This class is called a Pre-Ranger course. These soldiers do a great deal of physical exercise. They learn how to patrol. They also learn how to ambush. They must be able to attack an enemy without being seen or heard.

Soldiers must pass a physical test before they enter Ranger training. This test includes running, push-ups, and sit-ups. During their training, Rangers run and do other exercises every day.

Trainees must learn how to patrol and ambush.

Trainees may have to crawl under barbed-wire fencing while training on obstacle courses.

During training, trainees also must pass a number of tests in the water. They must be able to swim while wearing all their clothes and carrying their weapons. They also must be able to remove their gear while swimming underwater. In one test, trainees enter the water wearing a blindfold. A trainee must remove his blindfold without losing any gear.

Trainees advance in their training after passing the physical tests. They learn how to use different weapons. Rangers use rifles, machine guns, grenades, and mines. Grenades are small bombs soldiers throw. Soldiers usually bury mines underground. Mines explode when stepped on.

More Intense Training

As training progresses, the physical part of training becomes more difficult. Soldiers train on obstacle courses. Obstacles include high fences, barbed wire, and muddy pits. Trainees have to climb over or run through these obstacles to complete the course. Trainees often are exhausted and covered with mud by the end of the course.

Soldiers in Ranger training also learn other skills. They practice parachuting. They learn how to fight with their bare hands. They practice reconnaissance missions. On these missions, Rangers learn how to gather information about enemy forces.

Trainees experience many difficulties during training. They are allowed to sleep only a few hours a day. For food, they eat Meals Ready to Eat (MREs). These small packages of food are dehydrated. This dried food can stay fresh for years. MREs are the type of meals Rangers eat while on missions. Ranger trainees also learn how to hunt small wild animals. They might have to eat such animals for food on missions.

Trainees who pass training at Fort Benning move on to Camp Frank D. Merrill in Georgia. At this camp, they go through mountain training. Trainees learn how to use ropes to rappel. Soldiers use this rope-climbing method to move quickly down a mountain or cliff. They also use it to lower themselves from helicopters. Rangers must be able to rappel while carrying all of their gear.

Trainees finish their training at Eglin Air Force Base (AFB) in Florida. This area is swampy and filled with snakes. The training here prepares Rangers for jungle missions.

Rangers practice using small boats for travel.

Soldiers learn how to avoid and treat snake bites. They also practice crossing swamps in small boats.

A Real Ranger

Trainees who complete jungle training are almost ready to become Rangers. But not all of these soldiers will become Rangers. Not everyone who finishes the course is considered qualified to be a Ranger. Trainees must also show that they can be leaders during missions. They perform missions to show that they can handle the pressures of combat.

The training continues for these soldiers. They practice parachuting. They go on marches as long as 30 miles (48 kilometers) long. On these marches, they carry packs weighing as much as 50 pounds (23 kilograms). Rangers also train in very cold or hot areas of the world. They must be ready to fight in any climate or weather condition.

Military Terms

AFB – Air Force Base

Barrett Sniper Weapon System – a rifle Rangers use to hit distant targets that are as far as 1 mile (1.6 kilometers) away

CRRC – Combat Rubber Raiding Craft; Rangers use these small rubber boats on rivers or in swamps.

Light Infantry – soldiers who carry all their own equipment and weapons; Rangers are trained to fight without the support of tanks or other large weapons.

MREs – Meals Ready to Eat; Rangers eat these packets of dehydrated food while on missions.

RAAWS – Ranger Anti-Armor Weapons System; this weapon system also is called a Carl Gustav after its inventor.

Ranger Handbook – a small book that tells Rangers how to survive in harsh conditions

SAW – Squad Automatic Weapon; Rangers easily can carry this lightweight machine gun.

Chapter 4

Weapons and Equipment

Rangers must move quickly. They do not carry heavy weapons. But they need weapons that are strong enough to fight enemy forces. Rangers' weapons are both lightweight and powerful.

Guns

Rangers use many different guns. One rifle they commonly use is the M-4. The M-4 can fire many bullets very quickly. Rangers can attach a a small grenade launcher to the M-4. The handle of this rifle also can be folded. This makes the M-4 easy to carry. Some Rangers also carry a Berretta M-9 pistol. Rangers use pistols when they are close to their targets.

Rangers carry all of their own equipment.

Rangers also use machine guns. These guns can fire bullets rapidly. The M-240 is a machine gun that Rangers use. Its bullets are attached to long belts. These belts are fed into the gun so it can fire quickly. Rangers also use the M-249 Squad Automatic Weapon (SAW). This machine gun is lightweight and easy to carry.

Sometimes Rangers need to shoot at small targets that are far away. They then use a special rifle called a Barrett Sniper Weapon System. Rangers can hit a target that is more than 1 mile (1.6 kilometers) away with this rifle.

Powerful Weapons

Rangers need powerful weapons to blow up enemy tanks and armored vehicles. Rangers may use the Ranger Anti-Armor Weapons System (RAAWS) for this purpose. This weapon system also is called a Carl Gustav. Gustav was the man who invented this weapon. The RAAWS is small. But it is very powerful. A Ranger holds the RAAWS on his shoulder.

Mortars help Rangers attack targets that they cannot clearly see.

The RAAWS fires shells that are about 3 inches (8 centimeters) wide.

Rangers also use mortars. These small cannons fire shells that look like small rockets. Rangers use lightweight mortars that are easy to carry. The mortar shells are more than 2 inches (5 centimeters) wide.

Rangers use mortars when they cannot clearly see their enemy. A Ranger scout moves forward to find the enemy. He radios the location of the enemy to the mortar team. The mortar team uses a small computer to aim the mortar. The mortar team fires at the enemy. The scout then tells the mortar team if they hit the target. If they did not hit their target, the mortar team adjusts the aim of their mortar.

Other Gear

Rangers sometimes use parachutes to reach battle sites. These usually are static-line parachutes. One end of the static cord is connected to the parachute. The other end of this cord is attached to the airplane. The static line pulls the parachute open when Rangers jump from airplanes.

Rangers also have tools that help them fight at night. One of these is AN/PVS-7 night vision goggles. Rangers attach these goggles to their helmet. Night vision goggles use light from the moon and stars to help Rangers see at night. Rangers can see up to 450 feet (137 meters) in the dark with these goggles.

Important Dates

1756 – French and Indian War; Rogers' Rangers form

1775 – Revolutionary War begins

1861 – Civil War begins; Mosby's Rangers are formed.

1942 – First modern Ranger battalions form

1951 – Rangers make first airborne attacks

1974 – 1st and 2nd Ranger Battalions form

1980 – Operation Eagle Claw; Rangers participate in the Iran hostage rescue attempt.

1982 – U.S. Army begins using the M-249 SAW

1983 – Operation Urgent Fury; Rangers take over an airfield in Grenada.

1984 – 3rd Ranger Battalion and Regimental Headquarters form

1989 – Operation Just Cause; Rangers capture more than 1,000 enemy soldiers in Panama.

1993 – Operation Restore Hope; Rangers help capture warlords in Somalia.

1994 – M-4 carbine rifle first used

Chapter 5

Future Missions

Rangers have performed the same type of missions for more than 300 years. But wars have changed greatly in recent years. Now, U.S. troops sometimes act as police forces.

Somalia
The United States sent troops to Somalia for humanitarian reasons. The United States wanted to help provide the citizens of this African nation with food and supplies.

Rangers acted as a police force in Somalia. They tried to catch criminals who were heavily armed. These criminals also prevented the United States from handing out food and supplies to Somalian citizens. The United

Rangers may act as a police force on special operations missions.

States was not at war with Somalia. But Rangers still fought and some died while performing their duty.

Special Operations

Some military leaders believe there will be no major wars in the future. They believe the U.S. military may perform more special operations missions such as in Somalia. Rangers will be needed for these missions.

The U.S. military will need Ranger units for special operations in the future.

Words To Know

ambush (AM-bush)—a surprise attack

infantry (IN-fuhn-tree)—soldiers trained to fight on the ground

insignia (in-SIG-nee-uh)—a patch worn by members of a group; the patch shows that all the members belong to the same group.

motto (MOT-oh)—a saying that states what a group stands for; the Airborne Rangers' motto is "Rangers lead the way."

paratrooper (PAR-uh-troo-pur)—a soldier trained to jump from planes using a parachute

rappel (ra-PEL)—to use a rope to move quickly down a mountain or from a helicopter

reconnaissance (ree-KAH-nuh-sinss)—a military task designed to get information about enemy forces

scout (SKOUT)—a person sent to collect information; Rangers often act as scouts.

To Learn More

Bohrer, David. *America's Special Forces.* Osceola, Wis.: MBI Publishing, 1998.

Koons, James. *U.S. Army Rangers.* Serving Your Country. Minneapolis: Capstone Press, 1996.

Landau, Alan M. and Frieda W. Landau. *Airborne Rangers.* Osceola, Wis.: Motorbooks International, 1992.

Internet Sites

Ranger Training Brigade
http://www-benning.army.mil

Ranger Regiment Association
http://www.therangerstore.com

75th Ranger Regiment Association
http://www.75thrangers.org/hq/hq1.htm

U.S. Army Center of Military History
http://www.army.mil/cmh-pg

U.S. Ranger Association
http://www.ranger.org

Useful Addresses

Ranger Memorial Foundation
P.O. Box 53369
Fort Benning, GA 31995

United States Army Infantry Center
Fort Benning, GA 31905

U.S. Army Ranger Association
P.O. Box 52126
Fort Benning, GA 31995-2126

Index